A CLEAR DROP

Praise
for
A CLEAR DROP

"Poet-artist, Cynthia West, takes us to "the place where we are all one bird...with no shoes for the journey." Here are poems from a multiple lifetime of catching lonely stars to polish into this brilliant, unmasked gathering of gifts. She may ask in her poem title "How Many Hands Can I Wave?" sharing with us her journey, a single clear drop of a searching light. Here a reader will become an uninvited guest to a solitary feast of keeping our dreams alive. Cynthia assures us we are alone, while inhabited by mountains, birds, rabbits and clouds.

—James McGrath, author of *Speaking with Magpies* and
The Sun Is A Wandering Hunter, both from Sunstone Press

"These poems testify that Cynthia West has been so present in the world surrounding her that her hand itself "is made of the valley, the mountain, the seasons." Likewise, is it the poet or quiet itself that "whisks the voice of the wind into the tea"? Reading her work gives us access to the world outside of our skin. These poems translate West's experience to the reader, a welcome excursion."

—Joan Logghe, former Poet Laureate of Santa Fe

"These poems arise out of a powerful, quiet generosity and hold the kind of wisdom that is wrought from living close to the earth as well as the human heart. They occupy a long breath; they are spacious. Within them is the "voice of the wind" and the mountains—a deep listening, inside and out. As the poet writes: "listen,/ no matter how fierce the wind." And we do. We follow the way meaning gathers in these lines; the breath and beat of wings and heart help us to see and hear anew."

—Renee Gregorio, author of *The Skins of Possible Lives,*
The Storm That Tames Us, Water Shed and Drenched

Also by Cynthia West from Sunstone Press

Rainbringer, Poems
The New Sun, Poems
In the Center of the Field, Poems

A CLEAR DROP

Poems

Cynthia West

SUNSTONE PRESS

SANTA FE

Sunstone books may be purchased for educational, business, or sales promotional use.
For information please write: Special Markets Department, Sunstone Press,
P.O. Box 2321, Santa Fe, New Mexico 87504-2321.

Body typeface › Californian FB
Printed on acid-free paper
∞
eBook 978-1-61139-383-5

Library of Congress Cataloging-in-Publication Data

West, Cynthia, 1942-
[Poems. Selections]
A clear drop : poems / by Cynthia West.
    pages ; cm
ISBN 978-1-63293-069-9 (softcover : alk. paper)
I. Title.
PS3623.E843A6 2015
811'.6--dc23

                            2015013514

WWW.SUNSTONEPRESS.COM
SUNSTONE PRESS / POST OFFICE BOX 2321 / SANTA FE, NM 87504-2321 /USA
(505) 988-4418 / ORDERS ONLY (800) 243-5644 / FAX (505) 988-1025

Dedicated to the Dreamers

"We are all here, in the generous kitchen
of the house where wings are mended.
Bird people are awkward on the ground
but we remember the high windy places
and we will reclaim the sky."

—"House of Four Hawks" by Robert Moss,
excerpt from *Dreamways of the Iroquois*

CONTENTS

FIRST STEPS

A REVOLVING DOOR

THE COLORS OF SEASONS

TOO QUICK TO HOLD

ACKNOWLEDGEMENTS

My thanks to the publications in which the poems, sometimes in previous versions, have appeared.

REVIEWS

"The Candles We Lit," "The Turning Point," "The Craving," *Malpais Review*, Winter 2012–2013

"With Mom's Ashes," "Abandoned Toys," "With Trust and No Sound," "To Be Free," *Malpais Review*, Spring 2014

"The Dream Eaters," *Santa Fe Literary Review*, 2014

PRIZE

"The Canyon Road Paint-out," The Santa Fe New Mexican Writing Contest, 2013, third place, adult poems

PREFACE

As a poet, I travel a different map, one with sand traps and tunnels that lead to clouds mirrored in mountain pools. Writing with pen and paper is my way of heeding the wordless ones who have much to tell. When morning light sighs, leaf veins gather water beyond ideas of line and form.

My hand is a nameless bird, dropping feathers that point to distances and heights. The lake which disappears at the touch reflects the enigma glimpsed through green lavender glass. I see as a child, window eyes wide with rain. Music runs onto the pages, unhampered by thought. Sometimes the stanzas breach like whales, huge upheavals that leap, swallow the sun, then plunge, full of light, to the depths.

This does not make me different, but more the same, a patchwork person collaged of the many who want to be heard. The only wrong turn would be to quit, overwhelmed by the impossibility of combining the cacophony of discordant flutes, the tweeting of sparrows hidden in thickets.

Straddling the mythic gap between the promise and the loss, I continue to allow the garden to hunt me, setting its lures, enticing the magic to surface. The turning of light and shade ticks away the minutes of my years. Kneeling among stalks, I dig my fingers down to tend the river of unborn poems. Silent friends below sight know my touch, the warmth, the patience it takes to wait.

At day's end, casting a long shadow, I climb home hauling water gathered to revivify the dust. The sky calls, a reminder I have never owned my breath, only participated in a great wind.
The drop enters, more clear than air, more simple.
I have never been summoned from so far.
I have never been held so close.

—Cynthia West
Santa Fe, 2015

INTRODUCTION

Cynthia West first treated me to an entry into her worlds in the autumn a few years ago. Her intent was that I should witness the harvest abundance in her garden near the source of the Santa Fe River. I was entranced by the way the gifts of nature and human industry complemented each other. Strolling around her land, I was able to soak up the bumper crop of hollyhocks and grapes, the many colors of flowers and vegetables.

She welcomed me to spend time in the earthen domed chapel she built in 1975 to serve as a dwelling for the Lady of Guadalupe, who stands as a potent influence in her work. I felt a sense of being a part of a living myth that stretched back centuries. A stillness prevailed at the intersection of her visible and invisible worlds.

Later, when we sat sipping tea in her arbor nestled above the fields, Cynthia said she has an instinctive recognition of the interpenetration of the mythic and the world of form. Then, she read a poem of a deer, significant to me because I'd been compelled by her embodiment of the animal. "Cynthia" is the birthplace on the Mount in Greece, of the moon goddess and huntress Artemis/Diana, a being of nature and lady of beasts, a deer woman fiercely defending her birthright.

Her new elemental volume offers an invitation to partake of the crossroads in this realm. A banquet is in store for you! She offers abundant nourishment and visions from imaginal and sensual expanses. Inescapably, it feels like entering into a native experience, a precious glimpse into the diurnal round of the first person in the world, recounting the unfolding of seasons, the opening of buds and the revelation of life. Her presence in the cycles of nature dissolves separateness into multiple receptors of bounty, allowing you to traverse formerly uncharted territories.

The visual richness of her images is expected, yet there are also intimations of music throughout: in Too Quick to Hold, she bursts into a full symphony of instruments and sounds. "Hear the wind playing music with the birds." To me, this is truth rising from her ability to witness in silence.

In the section "Black Butterfly," Cynthia, like Orpheus before her, has been intrepid in tracing movements through the underworld with breathtakingly dark intimacy and despair. She has prepared the reader for the touch of the clear drop that enters through crevices or flows from above, providing emergence and return. This moment invites "The flutes they raised for the wind to sound."

She shares an original vision as she moves through this life, on a canvas broad enough to encompass even the stars. We experience surprise and wonder as she leads us into vast territories and shows us how to navigate, "to grab the mane of the white wind mother."

A Clear Drop addresses the powerful and mythical in our present world. This eloquent book of poems is a reminder of how much we have, and how much we could lose if we neglect these presences.

—Ann Yeomans
Archetypal Therapist
Santa Fe, 2015

FIRST STEPS

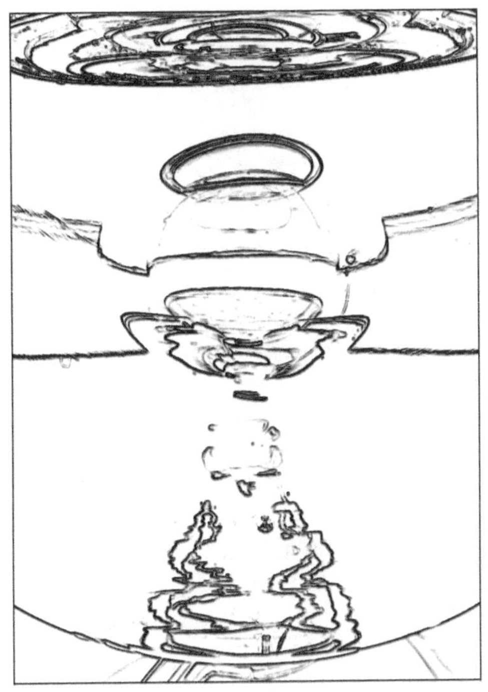

Not Knowing the Forms

Sitting at the loom, I catch
        the first ray of the year. It will lead
        the threads to come. In the time
        of deep cold, I ask the mountain

for the quiet to weave the strands
        of my days into the vertical warp
        strung taut between earth and sky.
        My fingers twine the red blood

of sunrise, the soft dust of footprints,
        the black of long moons waiting.
        I wind in the unheard rustlings
        wild grass roots dream during

their winter's sleep. With golden stalks,
        with grey twigs, with white snow,
        the patterns begin, not knowing
        the forms events will make of them.

It is gladness to sit, a solitary dove
        at the dawn of the year,
        passing the first fibers in and out,
        tamping with the beater.

Little Baby Pearl

Little baby Pearl, fresh from the womb,
born with the apricot blossoms,
you remember the hallways the sun walks
in praise. Under your skin the golden flame
burns clear as water, singing
without end. Your lips on your mother's breast
drink from the ocean of milk. After winter months
of gestation, you have unfurled, secure
in the great branch. Although the April wind gusts,
your petals know better than to let go.

Little Pearl, filled with the unseen,
the elixir shines in your eyes. With the sprouts,
you have thrust through the stones and the earth.
New air expands your delicate lungs,
clean windows open a view
that smiles beyond this hour.
Always remember how to find
your home in the first morning.

Remain in the love
with which night surrenders into day.
Breathing, beating, always sing
your vow. Close to the mountain, the moon,
the field, you are the same green flame
as the grass tips rising. Hear the wind
playing music with the birds. Listen with the sky
to the fire at your center. Never forget,
little Pearl beyond price. Never forget.

A Clear Drop

Before you remembered,
        your days were tangled nests,
        a beadwork of confusion,
        woven with no sense.

Although it is easy to forget
        the great gears of the stars,
        wheels upon wheels,
        when a clear drop enters,

it reminds your eyes to meet the roots,
        to know the flowers, the trees,
        the spaces where doves rest,
        cooing to the moon.

The wind's tracks might lead you
        anywhere. Follow the earth's
        advice. Pass through rain
        the way that mountains breathe it.

You are the simplest river,
        the wonder walked
        with nothing underneath,
        the ancient turtle that returns the sun.

Broken Foot

One bed, a thousand views.
I lie with my foot up.

November drab – a mask
that disguises mother of pearl.

The cat refused to be stroked
until she became old.

The ash branches, naked of leaves,
allow the magpies to discuss.

The fields sink toward sleep.
Flies buzz predicting snow.

In dreams, strong feet walk
searching for my beginning.

Morning shows me what I haven't found,
saying, "Start here, in this room, again".

Another day in bed, bare as the ash tree
and as filled with birds.

Your First Steps

The moon rising through sleep
sings the sound of surf,

here, then gone. Easy to believe
you never heard. Overhead,

the clouds and the stars
recognize the lunar butterfly

opening outside of time,
humming a ladder to earth.

The ears of the mountain,
understanding your journey,

listen to your first footsteps
walking the silver road.

A Broken-winged Bird

An empty skin with no name,
        I fell through canyons
        on a night without paths,
        in a wind with no breath.

The coyotes laughed.
        The crows cawed
        in recognition of my blackness,
        soot from the lost fire.

With a dust filled mouth,
        no words, no sight,
        I found company
        in a broken-winged bird.

Bright eyes with large pupils
        searched for mine.
        In my palm, a thirst
        I quenched by bringing water.

Held in Gestation

When the places
the road was going vanish,
what am I doing, standing on it,
a mannequin with no direction.
Every corner turned
leads somewhere
I don't know. Polished to satin
by the kisses of a thousand winds,
my transparency allows
everything to hurt. With no walls,
no fences, unable to stop people
from devouring me,
I ask the mountain,
"How long?"

Without the clothes of certainty
not much is left to walk upon.
What makes me suppose
I'm moving when I'm held,
stationary as a bead
on a wire?
Held, despite my wandering.
Held.
Held, until I stop.

Dragonflies

People who don't appear
to be doing anything
may be more productive
than we know.

Theirs is the true work,
the gathering of meaning
from the largeness
that words can't enter.

With faith in the crickets,
they lean on their hoes
gazing at the clouds.
With trust in themselves,

they stand beside the laundry
reading messages the wind
drops from the branches.
People who don't appear

to be doing anything
are wombs where seeds
and eggs merge in warm salt,
the blue gestation

which produces breath.
In their gardens, dragonflies
with strumming wings
hover to drink at the pond.

The Patience It Takes

When no one calls
and nothing happens,
I watch the sunlight walk

across the wall. I count
the shadows of grape leaves
tumbling, one by one.

When November freezes
calendulas to grey rust,
my aloneness is not alone

but the field where visions
grow in nests. Kneeling among
wind-rattled stalks I dig

my fingers down to tend
the river of unborn poems.
The silent roots below sight

know my touch,
the warmth, the patience
it takes to wait

in the quiet
of the empty garden,
as the new moon rises.

The Blue Wound

The grey before sunrise
is a blind medicine woman

tossing a kestrel
from the ash trees

on the western edge
of the field. She casts it

directly over me,
marking my forehead

with its shadow,
a blue wound

that penetrates. My eyes fill
with the slowness

that turns stones
into sand. A new valley

unfolds luminous tracks
for me to follow

to the place
where we are all one bird.

The Smell of Rainbows

Among wild sunflowers,
it isn't possible to locate the edge

between my skin and the sky. Shadows
of thunder racing over the mountain

change color at every glance.
I am not only the valley nestled in the clouds

but the dawns, the new born deer.
Many of my faces have ripened, fallen,

returned to earth. I am the loved ones' ashes
resting in the field, furrows the wind

soothes with fingers of rain. In the river,
round white pebbles breathe the light.

In my veined hands, the smell
of rainbows, crushed mint, basil, coriander.

There is no need to block
the stars pouring from my eyes.

An Agate Music

If I watch without looking,
the edge where the sky

meets the red cliff
opens a crack. Willing to hang

suspended in emptiness,
I slide through

into the clay of origin,
a large country, blue

with mountains.
The well-spring in my veins

is an agate music
remembered from the womb.

I am formed
by the small things

I have held in my hands,
the smooth white stones.

I am formed of all the times
I've disappeared.

A REVOLVING DOOR

A Revolving Door

A stone with a hole in it – go through –
        to a stage. Follow the chalk steps,
        act the script as if it isn't turning
        into another view. Unfamiliar,
        each new character you are called to be.

 Count the sky for names.
        Patience waits in a polished onyx jar.

The stage, a stone with a hole in it –
        follow the chalk footprints,
        act the script as if it isn't turning
        into another view.

The path stops at the edge of the stage.
        The mailman will deliver you
        from being in between. He will put
        your letter in a box. Someone will open it,

read about the stage with foot steps
        blown from change to change.
        Someone will suppose you live
        in a revolving door. As the moon

returns, the hole in the stone
        shows a new other side, another
        unskilled beginning, another stage,
        steps drawn in chalk.

Daring to Cross

In the winter I gather sun seeds,
sow them in white snow. Stone horses

sleep in the valley, undisturbed. Because
I can't live outside in the cold, I discover

places no one is able to see. When ice
has opened the boundaries, the familiar

runs to hide. In the winter I travel
the spaces where no leaves remain.

With wide arms I wrap the sky around me,
asking for nothing, listening

to the stories night tells. Because the earth
is frozen, I tend visions, ripples raising

shackled wings, bread I leave for those
who follow. In the winter, I cross

the bridge, enter the field
of rainbows where wild ducks

dive reflected clouds for minnows.
They explain what I cannot.

Under the Snow

When the roofs are white with frost,
        cries without hope of response
        rise with the chimney smoke.

Requests that don't dare
        to come right out and ask, hang,
        frozen in the fog. The mud is marked
        with the tracks of drab birds,
        chances not taken.

It looks like no one is home
        but under the snow, grass tips burn.
        Unseen in the mornings,
        there are many of us,
        unheard, unapparent as clear ice.

Out of respect, we hold silence
        as the storms roll by.
        No one notices as we build
        worlds of light and color
        despite the invisibility that keeps
        our smiles from being seen.

In the time and place of all possibilities,
        the full moon horse runs
        when we call, hooves kicking,
        breath white as the wind.

The Night Book

Torn membrane –
enough space
for the spark to leap.

Only the wing prints
of mad moths
can describe the flame.

Bones burned to soot,
lunar reflections –
the pages that can't be seen.

After the crow passes,
the slicing sound,
loud in still air.

Old one – fishing with a stick,
your hook might catch
the shadow of the moon.

Wearing white robes
ebony lilies shout,
unheard.

Charred trumpets weep,
left on the door-step
by the rain.

The night book –
when it is understood
hidden wings can soar.

Raven Tracks

When he has raked the leaves,
lit the hearth fires, cloud trails

gather 'round. They can't be seen
unless he leaves his head on a stone

by the river. Cedar branches,
raven tracks, moon paths, hide

in the shadows. This is where he feels
his way through shifting browns

and blues that give no maps. Small turns
lead nowhere. His nerves, violin strings

stretched to resonate on willows,
follow the sound of colorless rain.

Clear water travels, breathing in and out,
air, mist, sky, past the highest peaks,

too far for birds. He would not know
I travel here as well, unless we meet.

Although You Didn't Know

Slipping between the morning
and the sunlight, I find pictures carved
on the cliff. Written characters mingle
with gnarled roots.

Sinking into the cloud language
that runs beneath the stream,
I join the beavers building tunnels
of reflections. Red-winged blackbirds
balance atop rushes warbling
liquid notes to late October.

On earth soft with pine needles
I spread my mat of woven grass,
my tea bowl, whisk, serving instruments.
Although you didn't know you were invited,
I welcome you to the dappled grove.

It is quiet whisking the voice of the wind
into the tea. It is yellow-leafed autumn
that swirls in the bowl. It is the mountain
slowly rising that I offer you to drink.

Up the Canyon

Concentric circles
        spread and dissolve after one duck
        arches its neck, dives. The light

has paled since yesterday.
        Silver ripples ride the moon's footsteps,
        reminders of the polished undersides

of wings. River willows reflect
        invitations to submerged currents,
        rides on the shadows of clouds.

Unnoticed piles of stones prove
        the patience with which one season
        succeeds another. When the wind blows,

the colors slide. With every breath
        the grasses fade to dry gold.
        In the tea gardens of the coyotes

gnarled pines overhang stones.
        The trail has disappeared,
        as has the end of the sky.

Her Amber Eyes

The highway, strewn with trash,
glows from the song the sun chants
as it vanishes in the west.
Ravens, suddenly gold, squabble
over shreds of meat.

The splendor forces me to park,
to step out. Trucks speed north
on 84, cabs, wheels, illumined,
drivers shining messengers
delivering abundance.

A coyote greets me, unafraid.
I return her grin, wondering
why she doesn't flee.
In her amber eyes,
her hunger, her fierce fire.

After she disappears
among the roadside weeds,
I beg her to return, bring her pups
to roll in the radiant dust,
to give me her wildness again.

The Dream Eaters

Rabbits, grey under twigs, quick as dusk,
        race the new moon west, vanish in shadow,
        fur paws and black-tipped ears. Born of starlight

in the arroyo, they grow overnight. By morning,
        fat from eating dreams, they tumble
        in the parking lot, eyes bright from running.

Rabbits stand, one on another, forming
        a bridge to the moon. When it swells
        to fullness their faces join its smile.

Revolving like a ferris wheel, they circle
        from mind to mind, giving back the dreams
        they have shined and polished.

Finding My Way

Auspices, like the blue arch of day,
	are ten-thousand transparent flowers.
	Heeding their voices,
	my feet find their way forward
	knowing who they are,
	who they touch.

Each white stone, each hope,
	muddy with years
	of coming and going,
	offers directions.

THE COLORS OF SEASONS

One Tear

As I travel, my stone is whittled away.
        A new body begins to appear, too naked
        to be understood. In the house

at the edge of the stars, my heart
        changes shape every day, sloughing off
        old skins, the forms I was taught

to believe. Visions burn blue along
        frozen ridges, luring my face to meet
        the moon of underground flowers.

Silver fingers repair my wounds,
        for there is not much time
        to wake up before destiny unrolls

the ball of string I must follow
        to water the roots of my tree.
        One tear will be enough.

The Green Stone

Who waits inside, counting the steps
until a momentary flute
releases sky blue melody?

Who removes masks, layer by layer?
Who peels down to raw bone
to read the stories tattooed beneath the skin?

Who weaves their own tale, placing
prayer after prayer, laying a house
that will stand for thousands of years?

Who begs for more voice to ask the air
the reason it is clear? Who lives in
an empty hall, simple as plain white cloth?

Who lies singing in the orchard grass?
Who finds the small, green stone hidden
on the highest shelf?

Who follows their ball of string
where they were told to go, beyond
the wind-blown hummingbirds?

The Shawls and Blankets

Reaping the colors of seasons,
I dip my yarns, hang rainbows to dry
from the vegas along with blue corn,
chiles, oregano, mint and basil.

I accept the shawls and blankets
of my years, the ones with rips, flaws,
unraveled sleeves, the ugly times when
hate worked the loom, when the patterns

couldn't meet. I savor the fragrance
of posole cooking for days on the stove,
the feast set and shared, apple pies,
paper bowls, tamales, beans, tortillas.

In the quiet between winter storms
I welcome the deer moving in me,
graceful hooves, bodies of roses,
antlers crowned with evergreens.

So, Eat

My two year old grandson, sheltering
        under my jacket, watched gusts of wind
        roar through the plaza, spirits unleashed
        by the thousand dancing feet,
        the evergreens, the drum calling rain.

Bombarded by piercing grit, gum wrappers,
        plastic bags, we raced for shelter
        in a home where gentle faces welcomed us
        to a table laden with food. "So, eat",
        they said, hands on aproned hips,
        eyes sharp to make sure we took a lot.

We loaded up on fresh-baked bread, deer meat
        simmered in red chile, posole, lime jello
        with marshmallows. Drinking Kool-ade
        of every color, we piled potato salad, prune pie,
        biscochitos on paper plates, feasted
        to the fullness that bursts the clouds.

While the waters thundered from the sky,
        it was belonging that we ate, sitting
        in the crowded kitchen, the ground
        shaking from the pounding feet,
        the room throbbing with the songs.
        We took in what it means to have enough.

Wedding Present Song

We dance up the peaks of four colors.
We sing with the voices of canyons.
We gather the thunders in baskets.

Planting our staffs, we pollinate
the veins of the mountain,
our feet rooted in the first day.

We are the deer, antlers upholding
the sun, horns circling the disc
from which the light pours down.

Flanked by wedding vases and blankets
we sway with the kernels, the tassels,
we grind white corn to fill the bride's bowl.

Pure water we pour, that the couple will drink.
That they will grow old flying with eagles,
walking with bears, following the arrows

carved on ancient stones. We wrap
their bodies in the sash of the horizon.
Together, with one waist, their feet enter

the dance that the butterflies know.
In the palms of our hands we hold them,
until their return to the river of sky.

Through the Ice Naked

We enter the sweat lodge without
        our profits and losses. Leaving the moon
        outside in the wild plum thicket,

we melt in the burning steam, merge
        with a brighter light in the dark. The finches
        and the stars have heard our songs

for so many years they join in,
        as do the cedars in the sleeping fields.
        Tears summon a river to pour

through our bodies washing
        us clean. Where nothing can be seen
        it is clearer than glass;

it is night roses ringing bells. We drink
        the flood, the pain, the grace, finding refuge
        in arms that are fields of corn

under blue skies. Warm threads weave
        our brokenness into new flesh.
        We emerge, lie steaming in the snow.

We Flying Women Need No Rescue Line

Not confined to the museum, we twirl,
        carved wooden folk-craft,
        blue, purple, red, yellow, green,
        black hair-wings long,
        eyes large to hold the moon. We spin
        around the tree of life, a pole of sound,

a song wrung from our bones by flutes,
        drums, cymbals, tambourines. Ribboned
        skirts sail out revealing naked legs,
        open mouths. Once we leap off, circling
        past return, there is no climbing back

on the pedestal atop a ladder. Together
        with the earth, we weave rivers
        of laughter, waters that feed
        the inside skin. Our audience

is formed of the faithful,
        rich in the colors and doves
        that don't show, those who give thanks
        in the midst of winter. Eagles in training,
        at any moment they will soar,
        to join in our swirling net.

The Canyon Road Paint-out

At the bell-sound, on a cold, grey morning,
fifty two artists have ninety minutes
to create. With easels, tubes, canvases,
they are already running out of time.
Feeling they've never painted the mountains,

the birds, they smile for photographs. It is brave to try
to lure the pearl rain onto a surface. How can they
express the verdant feeling rising from the hills?
Brushes seek the true colors of the sky,
the day, the valley. Traffic roars, trucks,

buses, cars, people hanging out the windows
with cameras. It seems the whole world wants
what they promise on this small road
of mud houses. The minutes dissolve, rushing
with the sound of tires on pavement, hue by hue

becoming tree trunks, door-ways, fences.
Silver, the uncatchable clouds, wild horses
too quick to be ridden. With eyes all over
their bodies, mouths tasting each chartreuse leaf,
they drink the unseen sap that flows

the paint into meaning. Standing chilled
before their easels, they generate the event
that everyone came for, the view
that has no price, that lives unnoticed
in this dusty town. Passers-by, stopped

in their tracks, savor something more
than shadings of light and dark,
greener than the thunder sounding.
The bell rings completion. Wondering what
happened, the artists release brushes, paints.

The incomplete sketches
carry the morning.
People will bid on them,
hang them on distant walls,
ladders to what can't be told.

For Me to Discover

This morning the red cliffs taught me
        how to paint, not the booklet
        that came with the colors

or even the falcon that paused
        on a branch. The cliffs' friendship
        with the clouds, the cedars, the day,

how they waved their hands
        in accord with an invisible drum,
        informed my brush. The cliffs

have saved the names of the moons
        and the suns since before time learned
        to count. They held them for me

to discover when I entered their hues,
        terra rosa, purple madder, indigo,
        burnt sienna. Until they led me

down their roots, I couldn't imagine
        how the cliffs sought the core, pumped
        underground water. The flutes they raised

for the wind to sound summoned
        the bear of the stars to bring me the honey
        of earth, colors, trees and sky.

My Teacher

to James McGrath

Knowing I would need the wind
     to gather the clouds in paintings
     you spread the table

with ink ground black from the nights
     of no stars, brushes crafted
     in Tokyo with feathered strokes,

papers collected long and far away,
     blank dreams awaiting wing-beats.
     Demonstrating calligraphies,

rainbow, bird, lightning, friend,
     you taught my laden brush
     to race the sky.

Dancing Frogs

My Dad spoke in paintings
        of singing flowers, dancing frogs,
        the mushroom that bore me to earth

when I was born. He drew boats
        with laughing tuna, jitterbugging elves.
        I was the only one who knew

how to enter the colors, to play
        with him, to drive the bright red
        and blue train under the yellow sun.

We pulled the rope, sounded the whistle
        to warn my Mom as we raced
        around the kitchen way past

the speed limit. Having only words,
        she never got it, just felt left out
        that she couldn't follow us

into the sunflowers' smiling leaves.
        It was our secret. Not that
        we didn't invite her. She had no way

to come in. Now that he is gone,
        I have his paints, his fishing net, his frogs,
        his boat. We play and play and play.

How Many Hands Can I Wave?

Have my morning songs gathered
to form the path I walk?
When I sing a new one,
does my direction change? After so many,
can I utter one true to the shadows
rippling on the wall? Am I a stuck record
or the silence grasses speak?

How many hands can I wave in thanks
to the earth? May I taste the summer nectar
hoarded in the honeycombs of breath?

Loosed to dance at last, where will I find
the steps? Can the wind be my partner,
weaving in and out of the piñon trees?
Will my drum keep rhythm
in the dark of the moon?

Can I lay the hours into patterns
which are roadways for the promise?
How many birds am I carrying
on my shoulders? As I whirl
will they too awaken into flight?

The Crickets

Thanks to the crickets
under fallen logs,
to their small bodies
that keep the night turning.

TOO QUICK TO HOLD

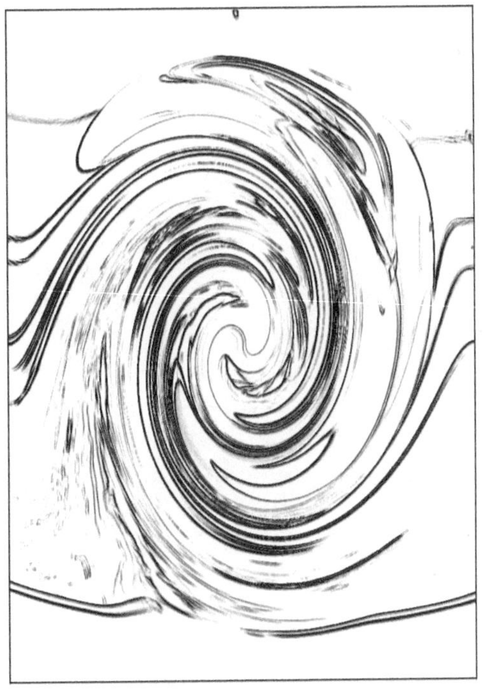

Heavy Going

Hoping to forge a way for those who follow
I climb the mountain under the morning star.
The dawn animals give me colors

to mark the path. Their bright eyes see through
my clothes to the trust I've broken,
the kind that can't be repaired. Traveling roads

in confusion, black, grey, dun, it is heavy going
with strings pulling in all directions. I've searched
since birth for the map I know. Mourning

my children, stolen while I pursued false trails,
I wash my ears in the hues of rivers
to learn the language of truth. There is no quiet

on the wrong track, burdened with mistakes.
Digging down to where the stars in my eyes used to be,
I release them to view the route that is clear.

Patience Waits

My ancestors brought me here
      to unpack the mask
      they made for me to wear.

I re-glue the straps, add new leather,
      attach evergreens to the antlers
      with blood-red twine.

The mask is their herd of wild horses
      running. It is the mountain.
      It is the candles they have waited

to light in me. It is the river of their tears
      rushing across the centuries,
      the water they give me to drink.

Patience waits in the earth
      gathering fallen music
      with rustling hands.

The White Wind Mother

Balancing a pole
        with a dark moon on either end,
        I tread a tightrope.
        The audience gawks
        at my night shoes sliding
        across a filament stretched

from one side of their minds
        to the other. A wobble
        in concentration forces my hands
        to grab the mane
        of the white wind mother.

Safe, riding in her warmth,
        I understand there is no need
        to put on a show
        built of wishes and stars.
        Her eyes, roads into the sky,
        are my own.

Too Late Now

When the west-wind scours
dust from stones,
it inflates my flesh to rise,
a helium balloon, rotund,
a red ball nose, spangled breasts.

Lifting off its precious tether,
my rummage sale personality
ignites high above the rainbow cliffs.
Ravens gawk as I cartwheel,
teasing solar flares. Scolding

my motley progress, they demand
I return to my role: a dead fish
on a plate. Too late now.
I'm beyond the cowering broom,
the well-scrubbed steps.

With my clown suit expanded
to fill the sky, fingers, toes,
like sausages about to burst,
I mount dusk's wings, chase
my shadow over moon-lit hills.

Grabbing a rattle of stolen bones,
I shake until it turns into a pair
of huge, round glasses, the kind
with a false mustache attached,
a jutting nose. Binoculars,

they magnify possibilities,
expose lost dreams. The west wind
blows, deflating my balloon.
Through the soles of my feet
the air smells of sudden rain.

Too Quick to Hold

My large hotel has chances staying in the rooms.
Tolling bells demand I not neglect their smiles.

If a musical scale measured the temperature,
it would be floating oboe, silver schools of change.

Every way I peel the surface, it's a hall of reflections.
The mirrors disclose the chances no colors can match.

What chance leads me to oil my parts with rags,
to collect saxophones I haven't the patience to play?

This river can't be kept from running past my hands.
When light shines on a change, it is too quick to hold.

The road I tread is a sheet of hand-blown chance.
Holding my basket, I gather summer flying south.

My fingers touch a broken doll, buried in the ground.
It may not be too late for the chance of laughter.

Flickers in the ash tree nest, wet, cold with rain.
Dark changes hidden in feathers incubate the eggs.

Chancing exposure, I find the hues I sought.
It is too late for promises. I must offer you a feast.

Praise to your friendship which completes me,
the chance which shines on my face like the rain.

Abandoned Toys

Walking in a plain coat among the piñons,
    I meet a woman who creates masks,
    her face haunted with stories.
    Joined in the sadness of each other's eyes,
    we share cast-off spoons, shoes,
    watches, wallets, flutes and fetishes.

Fascinated with abandoned toys,
    how their arms and wheels fit into forms
    that move, we coax the disparate parts of
    rubber gloves, hats, spatulas and spectacles
    into vessels that hold relief.

We collect rusty tears with tweezers,
    fill transparent tubes to use as arteries.
    For the flesh, we stir buried hoards
    of books with salt and trust,
    spread the mixture onto bones.

Two friends, among sheltering art
    forged from the unwanted, we watch
    storm crows vanish in the sun.

Hand in Hand

With no shoes for this journey, we nest
at the edge of beginning, grown old
in our skins. Our albums are thick
with photos of the tears we planted in clay,
tended until green sprouts flowered.

Loves we have lost, will you enter
one at a time so we may know you,
or are you the horde reflected
in the lakes of our eyes? If we plunge
in to reach you, ripples vanish

in the reeds. Water under our hair,
your flow with no border, no map,
is a falling upwards hand in hand,
an abalone shell, a delicious curve
in varied colors. Today there is no tree

that does not sing. Holding freedom
between us, we've forgotten how
to gather faults. Breathing the silk
that shines bare branches, we bloom,
hyacinths in the dead of winter.

Road Trip

Highway billboards display open doors
        through which we drive north
        to the clouds. Over the years

we have grown together, building
        small bridges for carrying corn
        to feed the nights of winter moon.

Traveling with our fingers intertwined,
        there are no boundaries. As we play
        the glass guitar, the piñons join

our wing-filled chords. If we could listen,
        the sentinel stones with eyes
        would offer us their vision,

the sight not stopped by any form.
        As we race along the desert,
        our stories unwind behind us,

deer tracks in the dust, shrines
        with golden bones, villages sinking back
        into the earth from which they rose.

January Stones

The days fly in formation, families of birds
        above muddy fields. Traveling Highway 25,
        photographers with lenses too short
        to catch the snow geese, we try ropes, jars,

language, maps. Having always gathered
        stones, we wouldn't survive a moment without
        their weight. More and more I understand
        how bravely we greet each other every morning,

how we say the same goodnight, how stuck
        we are in the routine of Monday,
        the laundry, Tuesday, the trash. Side by side
        in our car as usual, we follow the migrations

down the road but never all the way. Afraid
        to speak the truth, we admire the people who can,
        who accept their stones just the way they are
        instead of wanting better ones.

The Candles We Lit

When I don't have you, my dreams are scrolls
        with no brush strokes. On the last dark days,
        the low sun glares in the windshield,
        ignites the icy road. Rushing in different

directions we disagree, holding hands
        over squinted eyes. The candles we lit
        at the feast of lights have lengthened, revealing
        foundations built when we were friends.

Snow watches the table, the evergreens,
        our footsteps, the traffic, the slush.
        Now that you're here, I pay no attention
        to your talk, the words I wanted when you

were gone. The night pages open, charcoal grey
        with rust-stained seams. Unfolded, they release
        moths to fall flattened in my palm,
        silver dust, wing prints on vellum,

tracks of our vanished years. As another storm
        approaches our small house
        built of candles and coins that could be bright,
        it is not too late to stand together in the cold.

Winter Highway

Two strangers walk in me.
        One travels the brightness
        between snowflakes. One moves

with the ravens on a dark road.
        We board a bus
        without guessing its destination.

Sitting in the back,
        water dripping from our boots,
        we watch the storm waves

mingle with our words,
        unconcerned about the dangers
        of speeding over ice.

The driver knows
        how memories unwind
        during long winter journeys,

how the windows only seem
        to be closed. Hurtling down
        the interstate, my shining self

and my dark start singing
        the same song to the cadence
        of the tires. Across the fields

houses blink on and off,
        our differences, vanished
        in the speeding night.

The Monastery Pond

to Sister Miriam Randall

Rowing through the cat-tails
    in my indigo boat, I hunt for eggs
    laid by the night. Black ripples
    on black water hide whispers

which can only be heard
    in the tracks of the moon.
    Fingers searching
    the bottom mud touch a form

that can't be spoken
    pulsing in the shadows.
    With utmost care my hands lift
    a curving shell that warms

in response to my breath,
    sends forth a sound that melts
    the darkness into day -
    the sun fills my empty boat.

The Apple Fiesta

Today the parade sets out
    holding carrots in every hand,
    all the pennies saved, the gladness,
    bread and chocolate, way out of bounds.
    Don't hesitate, light all the candles.

Dusty Cerro Gordo Road
    becomes a green river, welcoming
    buoyancy. Trees shine, pouring pears
    into long-awaited pies. Terrors sleep
    among hollyhock seeds,
    twined in little bark nests.

The crickets chant night and day,
    sounding the season that tumbles
    too fast to catch. The sky hazes over,
    ash limbs blow, reclaiming September
    for the sun-drunk bees.

This afternoon celebrants wearing
    spiral hats join the rabbits cheering
    rain-rich thunder. The apples murmur
    with their leaves, a call and response,
    a shelter for listening fruit.

The Circle We Planted

We built a secret shrine with stones and rusted cans
       under the piñons in the arroyo. You were small then
       but large in belief. Now you run, kicking
       the anthills I taught you to respect. Someday,
       when you wise up, I will lead you back here.

With new eyes you will see the circle
       we planted, how it has sent roots, spread branches.
       With listening ears you will hear
       the kindness of the wind, the canyon murmuring
       our names, our names braided together
       with the grass blades we gathered,
       our names passing the hidden gift along.

The Promise

Unraveling the sky, I weave it
        into a new fabric to warm you,
        a coat blue with space
        and the promise
        that stars hide at dawn.

Tip-toeing back to bed,
        I cover you with it
        so I can watch your smile
        when you awake.

BLACK BUTTERFLY

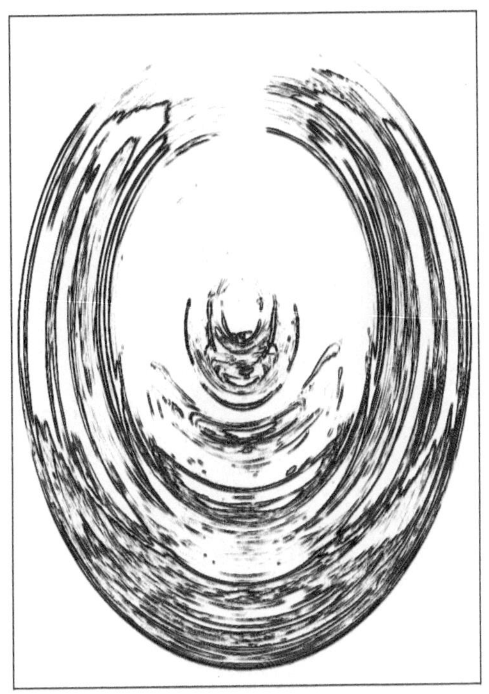

No Measure

The wind blows hard every day,
pushing the clouds loose.

With my mouth sealed
against prayer, I can't travel
with the falcons that carry requests
to the message stone.

The crops wither. I have broken
the water jars.

With my face in the dust,
I beg for the hands
to make a new bowl.

There is no measure
for the needs it must contain.

The Turning Point

The morning swerves sideways, irritating
       my restless edges. Hurting from lack of
       presence, I boil water, watch silver bubbles

surface, pop. Tea can't restore the vanished apples,
       the summer birds, the marigolds. Shaped for praise,
       childhood treasures have shrunk to snowy

cardboard squares. With eyes fixed on the wall,
       I forget to look out the window at my movie
       scrolling by, turquoise glass, flashing in the sun.

The everyday kitchen table is no longer mine
       any more than the tea, the light, the day.
       It takes confidence to sit by the stove,

to trust, to continue from one moment to the next.
       In the film, green wheat stands tall,
       only to dissolve in frozen fields.

Bitter Spring

No drops of rain
the sky has forgotten
the taste of water.

A black butterfly
hastens past frozen
cherry blossoms.

Ruined fruit
a friendless feeling
no fragrance.

The old adobe
counts one-hundred
dry springs.

Dust devils gallop
trampling stones
on the road.

New-hatched snakes
crawl back in stone walls
hoping for shelter.

Pansies' faces
bow toward the ground
sorrowing for warmth.

With Mom's Ashes

This morning in the clear light, gathered
      in the field with Mom's ashes
      in a plastic bag, each one of us is

thinking how little we've made use
      of our chances. The dry earth is held in the
      arms of the mountain. We are not so large,

standing under the hot sun. We can't pretend
      to own this day. The door between worlds
      opens while we reminisce, luring

our shadows over the threshold that leads
      to the moment. We bend, scoop
      the white dust of her burnt bones

into a crystal pitcher, move in a circle,
      take turns pouring. In the shining heat
      her particles dance, an unexpected snow

that arises, departs. As fast as we spread
      her remains the air draws them up,
      removing the traces. The round path

we are forming together will continue,
      reminding us to stand tall, to listen,
      no matter how fierce the wind.

The Stone Wheel

Wearing a path
     through the weeds,
     I walk the field every day
     carrying a shovel
     to bury my grief.

A cemetery of small tombs,
     white circles gone to dust,
     my parents' graves hold
     glass birds shattered too soon,
     flutes not played enough.
     Each mound lies watered
     by unseen tears.

In the center, the stone wheel,
     long ago painted bright yellow,
     red, blue. Scraps of color
     remain around the edges.
     It is too heavy to turn.

This morning, I dig another hole
     to contain the emptiness.
     Alone without the weight
     of my broken birds,
     I spread wild sunflower seeds
     upon the fresh-turned earth.

Nothing,

not the magpie lying on the driveway,
        blood pooled
        on the gravel beneath her beak,

not the ravens scolding through the clouds,
not the rain drops on the peach branches,

tells me how the bird,
        every feather perfect,
        died.

There is nothing to do
        but stand
        admiring the iridescent wings.

It is better not to ask
        the round black eyes
        staring sightlessly
        into mine.

The first ant climbs her chest.

In the Season of Ripening

This garden is where I'll die,
        a white moth
        among the nasturtiums
        and marigolds. I will not pass away

of an incomplete heart
        but from the fullness
        of hummingbirds. At once, I am old
        and young, quick as the silver storms

blowing through the minds
        of stones. In the galloping clouds
        there are hallways with rooms
        for each of us. Swallows soar

from the thunder's voice, weaving
        patterns across the sky. Accompanied
        by the morning star, my ears
        have learned to be quiet enough

to hear the the mineral hills.
        Young and old at once, I stand
        among the tawny rocks. The wind plows
        furrows in my face. Flash floods

carve arroyos through my flesh.
        With eyes burning like stars
        from tending the central fire,
        I have gathered many flowers for you.

In the Shadows

The death magnet, an over-sized moth
        with black eyes on its wings, casts a pall
        that shrinks the view. Bestowing

charcoal-hued sight, it plays a wounded cello
        tolling the end. Since yesterday's lightning
        the fire ants have sheltered inside

their crystal hills knitting pine needles
        toward the approaching cold. Dark ears
        listen for mice. In the shadows

of rusting leaves, the last hummingbird,
        wings whirring too fast to see,
        strums dirges to the frozen marigolds.

With Trust and No Sound
to Vivien Myerson

It is time you join the flock of pigeons
wheeling in the sun, wings first dark
then bright. Time you forget the known path,
let your feet run with the feathers

of the wind. Time to race up the mountain
you never allowed yourself to see. Time to welcome
the light into your movements so you can
turn with the seasons.

With your bare branches lifting,
there is nothing but space between the stars.

You've thrown your seed bag in the mud,
leaving the sprouting to chance.

When your breath disappears, the largeness
with no body takes your hand, guides you away
from plowing and weeding.

With trust and no sound the orchard
grows by itself.

It is time to fall through opening
after opening, with no need to be caught,
no need to be held.

Let Go

Just let it happen
the way ducks polish a pond
by diving and surfacing.

Unconcerned,
they trail wakes of sunlight
for the water to drink.

The hills neither create
nor control the piñons jutting
from red stone,
simply wear them
as smiles.

THE ONLY WATER

Here, Take My Hand

Although you walked this path every day
        you have been gone so many years the magpies
        have forgotten your name. My friend,

you no longer know the valley where you used
        to laugh, although it calls you as you bend
        spinning clay into beauty that gives joy.

Here I am, talking to the part you locked
        in a box one spring long-ago. You crafted
        the latch so strong none of us can undo it.

Now that you hurt, you want to find the key
        you hid, but not enough to ask where it is.
        Another year, I'm digging the earth, planting

the seeds. Waiting for you to be here, I hang flags
        you might like, if you looked up. Hearing
        your footsteps, I turn. Was it only the wind

or are you too sad to touch? Here, take my hand.
        It is made of the valley, the mountain, the seasons.
        It offers all you have lost.

Voices

In the night when nothing can be seen,
        waters from the deep ground
        rise up the trunk carrying stories
        to the tree. They murmur tales

from before roots sought wetness,
        before leaves drank air, before seasons
        tumbled down gold. Their voices
        are rivers bearing the force of storms.

Merging with the sap, their memories
        open mouths on the branches,
        eyes in the fruit. The tree wakes
        to the dawn, uttering green praise.

Shaking light and shadow,
        it mingles with the morning
        as if the hours were hands
        held together, meeting in silver rain.

A Child of the Mountains

Long ago, before time and sorrow,
        a dream bear ambled
        down a river-bed, her fur rippling
        with sun, leaf-dapple and wind.

The old cliffs witnessed
        as she summoned the bees
        to lead her to honey.

Shimmering was her hide,
        gold, her eyes. Inside her pelt,
        watch-fires edged the ridge-lines
        of the stars.

The clouds gave her songs,
        with faces painted
        in the four directions.

She rubbed red earth on her fur,
        coloring it human
        until she had a dancer's limbs
        and the hands to tell stories.

The mountain grabbed her,
        demanded her return. Unwilling,
        she sang the songs of the breeze.

When the leaves fell, her paws,
        remembering, couldn't help but follow
        the water-course back to her home.

Searching for You

Trekking dusty canyons, stumbling over stones,
losing and finding the trail, I follow wild verbena
and the cries of mourning doves. Your warmth

feels close as hawks glide thermals. Waiting for you
is not like anything, for you have less color than air.
Aeons ago, water carved this chasm. Wind polished

the stone. Is your presence hiding in the echo
of a moment I can't touch? Are you calling
in the hues sliding down the slopes, vanishing

with the changing light? When I sink exhausted
on a ledge, feet, arms, red with dust, you touch me,
stay only until recognized, then depart.

Among the Stalks

At three in the morning
	a mother deer and her fawn
	find the garden safe enough
	to rest their white bellies

beneath the pear tree. Sensing
	my approach, they melt
	into the dark. I press my body
	into their warm hollows

to learn the quiet they breathed.
	Nestling among the stalks
	where they praised
	the morning star reminds me

who wrapped the horizon
	to hold us upright, who painted
	our colors, who taught us
	how to mix them to make gold.

The Craving

Days like this when the wind casts trash
      on the road, when snow walks the mountain,
      the tamed ache breaks its chains,

runs amok, gnawing bones. The craving for relief
      chases me down the canyon, screaming for
      what can't be found. Calling my kin to appear,

I demand their round stone bodies assume features
      that look like mine. Crying for want
      of people who talk like me, I can't wait

for the friends who live in my blood
      just out of reach.

A dust-blown scrap of plastic bag,
      I land on a kitchen table
      with a checkered cloth. There are pears in jars,

the ones I put up, the same red and white labels,
      the same face, my own, welcomes me home
      to my warm kitchen. Outside, the storm roars.

In the dark of the moon, I will not forget
      my thankfulness again, no matter what.

The Red Hat

Needing a crown I can wear
        to live my best story, I search
        the Saturday afternoon flea market,

thousands of second-hand wishes.
        Skulls, tigers, devils, bulls,
        devas, nothing that can be set up

as a ladder to reach the light. My days,
        after being hidden in smallness,
        have emerged into celebrations

with vast firework displays. Dreams
        have forged my wing-bones
        into flutes. Among the piles of goods,

a phrase of jazz repeats. As the vendors
        cover their wares with blankets, time
        is running out to buy. Buried in the welter

of purses, bedspreads, silverware,
        the red hat calls. Gasping, I recognize
        its jeweled peony, two golden phoenixes

stitched of primal fire. On my head
        it is the mountain that flies, fueled
        by the ashes of winter's grief.

The One Who Can Answer

No wrong turns across the dreamscape
        when the man you invited
        with a hundred flowers

comes to visit. At last the other half
        of your tongue arrives, the one
        who can answer the side of your face

you can't see. He doesn't seem to mind
        your mouth taped shut, how you hold
        your hand over your shame. It doesn't

stop him from speaking in your thoughts.
        He climbs, tweed jacket, shoes and all,
        into your single bed, perfectly at home,

comments that the pillow is just right.
        How his brown eyes twinkle. Maybe you
        could let him see beneath the tape.

Maybe he came for you,
        just the way you are.
        Maybe you can't hide a thing.

The House Made for Me

For decades, a wind
        has pushed me west toward the setting sun,
        to the grass, the roses, the sea,

to orange trees preparing
        their night bloom. Whose hand built
        the door that is waiting

to be opened by mine? While moons
        ride dark waves, the house
        made for me lets nights sleep

in its empty white rooms. Smooth
        but for dead moths,
        the wood-plank floors beckon

the tread of my feet. Studio windows
        watch the road, shining with colors
        saved for my arrival. The deer

grazing these brown hills know
        I am here. The yellow-fin tuna reflect
        the stars, the shore, the salt currents,

the sound of a house no longer lonely,
        suddenly filled
        with the music of return.

Too Many Times

The snow blows sideways, eddies
        of rushing stars. Crows caw in the cedars,
        complaining we don't listen,
        that the only story we've been given

has succumbed to our neglect,
        that we've ignored the beauty
        we were formed of, clay, bones, blood,
        breath, tears. The feathers that could

teach us how to fly have been refused
        too many times. The dawn clouds
        of Our Lady's robes, salmon, ruby,
        peach, stain the winter fields.

She walks the canyon whispering
        our names. The salamander is nourished
        by Her rainbows seeping
        through the stones. Little black crickets,

folded tight as twigs, smile in their dreams
        at the sound of Her tread.
        Though we have run out of promises,
        She forgives.

The Only Water

The lily that you disguise demands
you let it unfurl. It hides yellow pollen, light
for the dwelling you deny. When will you
let yourself have what you want?

Your bones know where they belong.
Many cold winters you've been learning
to generate the only water
in which you can breathe.

Leave those visits to the locksmith.
You have kept yourself out
trying to be safe. You've been too busy
to swallow the flowers clouds drop.

Let the blue waves wash you.
The sea birds are calling your name.
Answer with your voice of breezes.
You can't guess the depth

of the well you've dug
until you look -
there is no bottom,
only stars.

The Central Rib

Does the grass teach me how to pray?
        What can the sun tell me of the blades,
        how they bend, how they dance,
        how they bow without the wind?

There are whole meadows, with more
        strands than I can count. Can I learn
        to be that many parts moving as one?

What about the green veins branching
        from the central tree? Is my axis
        the same rib that formed Eve in the garden
        long ago? Can I follow the fluids
        spinning up and down the stalk?

Will I drown in beauty, forgetting to gasp
        for air? Do the roots reach into the mouth
        of creation? Do the words thunderclouds speak
        kneel on the earth all day? Do they sing

praises to the moon? Does the wheat realize
        its wings? Is there any difference
        between an eye and a seed? How high
        must verdant stems ascend
        until their songs ring out?

To Be Free

is moving forward
along the edge between day and night
where trees dissolve into dark air.

is knowing you step where you mean to
despite the road being invisible
to all but rabbits and mice.

is remembering you have little to do
with the placement of your feet,
although you can minimize your tracks.

is to have the nakedness
not to wear other people's ideas,
even those you mistake for your own.

is to look past the comfort of surfaces
to the possibilities they cover.
The curved horizon is the mask of blue waves.

is to travel with the cottonwood float,
wind-borne, uncaring of direction,
destination, appearance.

is to be water ripples
running through one another,
interchangeable, uttered by birds.

This book of poetry is printed on acid-free paper.
The typeface is Californian FB

In 1938, Goudy designed California Oldstyle, his most
distinguished type, for University of California Press.

In 1958, Lanston issued it as Californian.

Carol Twombly digitized the roman 30 years later for California;
David Berlow revised it for Font Bureau with italic and small caps;
Jane Patterson designed the bold. In 1999, assisted by Richard Lipton &
Jill Pichotta, Berlow designed the black and the text and display series.